A Night of Rhythm and Mews

A musical extravaganza

A Night of Rhythm and Mews

A musical extravaganza

by

Fox and Marshall

RAINCLIFFE BOOKS

First published in 2023 by Raincliffe Books
Illustrations by A Fox. Words by R Marshall.
Copyright © Fox and Marshall 2023

The right of A Fox and R Marshall to be identified as the author of the work has been asserted herein in accordance with the Copyright, Designs and Patents Act 1988.

All rights reserved. This book is sold subject to the condition that it shall not, by way of trade or otherwise, be lent, resold, hired out or otherwise circulated without the publisher's prior consent in any form of binding or cover other than that in which it is published and without a similar condition including this condition being imposed on the subsequent purchaser.

All the characters in this book are fictitious and any resemblance to actual people, living or dead, is purely coincidental.

British Library Cataloguing in Publication Data
A catalogue record for this book is available from the British Library

ISBN 978-1-9161166-1-0

Typeset by Amolibros, Milverton, Somerset
www.amolibros.com

This book production has been managed by Amolibros
Printed and bound by T J Books Limited, Padstow, Cornwall, UK

This book was made forty years ago when a musical household welcomed the arrival of a darling new daughter and the story was developed as private amusement.

Now Raincliffe Books are pleased to make it available to a wider audience for the very first time…for all with a feeling for music and cats. It is of course a work of the imagination. Only Bruno the cat was real.

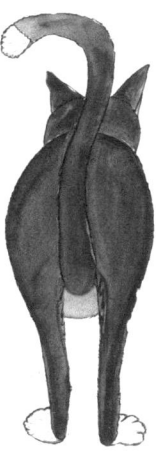

For Charlotte

Professor Percy Nightingale needed to think.
    All his life he'd told his students how great music should be written.
    Now at last he was ready to write some himself. Almost…
  Day after day he walked along his regular footpaths, listening to the world and listening to himself, but, try as he might, his mind was blank.

…Until…finally one afternoon, a strange sound came floating across from behind a wall. Percy Nightingale shivered in delight. He just had to find out what it was.

"As I've always said," smiled Percy, "the world is full of music. We just need to set it all free!"

Percy Nightingale was not really surprised to find a dustbin full of kittens but he was absolutely astonished to see that one little cat looked very much like his most famous friend, the great conductor, Bruno von Schnittlauch.

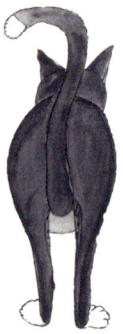

"Bruno!" cried Percy in amazement. It was the first kind word the little cat had ever heard. Now at last he knew who he was.

Professor Percy Nightingale was so delighted with the wonderful sound still ringing in his ears that he hurried straight back to his flat to write it down.

Bruno came too. As he sat by the fire, he began to purr for the very first time in his life. "Splendid," said Percy, "such a deep rich tone is just what we need.

"Absolutely purrfect!"

He smiled to himself at his own little joke and again he wrote down the notes.

For the rest of the afternoon, Percy worked on the opening to his new piece. His first proper composition had begun to flow at last.

When it was time for tea, he sat down by the fire to toast his teacakes. The kettle boiled. The teapot was filled.

Bruno had found a home.

Of course Bruno was not used to living in a flat and had a lot to learn.

He had to learn where NOT to sharpen his claws.

    He also had to learn where NOT to hide when Percy wanted to listen to his gramophone.

    Most of all, he had to learn NOT to let his gang of friends get their paws and claws into the neighbour's laundry box.

The Lady next door was never too pleased to find paw marks all over her sheets.

But Percy Nightingale was very forgiving and very cheerful because now his head was always full of music. Day after day he wrote it down as fast as he could.

Bruno tried his best to be helpful and so Percy continued to discover wonderful new tones and effects. He'd never imagined just how mysterious a piano might sound with the strings all smothered in fur.

The Nightingale score was very unusual and full of modern ideas. Certain passages were left to chance…others were left to Bruno. Somehow he always managed to put his paws down in just the right places.

By the time Percy wrote the very last note at the bottom of the very last page, his whole flat was covered in sheets of music. "Where has it all come from?" he wondered in amazement.

He bundled all the pages into a pile and very proudly wrote out the title. "***From Afar. An Extravaganza for Orchestra*** by Percy Nightingale."

A moment later he added underneath. "To Bruno in gratitude and admiration."

Percy smiled. Bruno began to purr. Their first great work was complete.

Meanwhile across the sea, Bruno von Schnittlauch was growing more and more bored. The great conductor had nothing to do. He had performed all the music he could find and nothing seemed to excite him anymore. Was this the end of a glorious career, he wondered?

Little did he know that a brand new score of a brand new piece was already in the post from his old friend in London. Percy Nightingale had sent one copy of his work to von Schnittlauch and another to the people in power – the men who held the money.

Long before rehearsals could begin, the Concert Committee had to meet and agree to pay the bills. Some of these famous men were Bankers, some were Lawyers and others were Academics who wrote heavy books.

All were experts, but nobody could claim to know more about music than Dr. Woodhead.

He was the Chairman of the Committee. He was also in charge of the Music College where Percy Nightingale worked so leadership came naturally.

"I don't like the look of this," he murmured, glancing at the first page of the score.

"***From Afar*** indeed! Poor Nightingale can't be well. The years must have taken their toll. The sooner we put him out to grass the better. I think I'll make him an offer he cannot refuse."

The Committee began to sweat. They coughed and shuffled. Quickly they voted to reject the work and went on to matters of money.

Professor Percy Nightingale was very upset. He'd never expected to lose his job.
For what might be the very last time, he climbed the stairs to the college practice room. Numb with shock, he stared out of the familiar window, thinking of all the students he'd known.

Some were very gifted and were now famous performers.

Others had to face a long hard struggle with little hope of success.

Who would help them search for hidden harmony now?

Worst of all, **From Afar** would never be heard. The world would never experience the wonderful music he carried in his head. He would just be ignored and forgotten like so many others before him.

Sadly, Percy returned to his flat.

Tea and toasted teacakes were totally forgotten. He put some of his favourite tunes onto the ancient gramophone, but not even "Stormy Weather" could drive away the clouds of dismay.

Meanwhile, across the sea, Bruno von Schnittlauch picked up his copy of **From Afar**. How delighted he was that his dear old friend Percy had finally finished such a hefty piece. "To Bruno in gratitude and admiration," he read. Despite all his successes, he was deeply moved.

(Never for a moment did he suspect that now there was another Bruno in the world of classical music.)

Turning the pages of the score, he became more and more excited. Here at last was a worthy tribute to his enormous talent. It was just what was needed to lift him out of his gloom. He was so excited that for once in his life he forgot his agent and personally phoned Dr. Woodhead to fix a date for the first performance…without even mentioning his fee.

But Dr. Woodhead was a Principal with principles and when he said, "No," he meant "NO!"

However, "No" was a word von Schnittlauch never noticed. After all, here was a man who owned one Opera House, two Skyscrapers, three Recording Studios and four planeloads of musical stars.

The Woodhead "No" was no more than the challenge he needed to bring him out of the swimming pool and into the gym.

Daily he recovered more and more of his old energy. Every morning he limbered up with the help of his greatest recordings. No Woodhead would get in his way!

But then he realised that a lot of his best players were away on tour. He'd sent them off to play all over the world until his gloomy mood passed. Without many of his trusted team, an immediate performance of **From Afar** would be a terrible risk. He couldn't wait…but maybe he would have to. It could take ages. Would Woodhead win after all?

The shock was so great that he flopped back into his pool and for hours he drifted round in a daze. He felt more depressed than ever. Then out of the blue came a jolly good idea. He sat up so suddenly he almost fell off his airbed.

"I've got it," he spluttered. "That's it…Extravaganza indeed. Let's bring in new talent, Fresh Blood. A recruitment drive, a training course. Even a resting actor might be tempted!"

So now the wonderful world of classical music would throw open the doors to everyone.

It was an idea as up to the minute as the music itself. His Marketing Team were delighted. Soon the full resources of the Schnittlauch Corporation swung into action.

Like all great conductors, Bruno von Schnittlauch knew how to get his own way. He wrote a few cheques, twisted a few arms, threw a few tantrums and turned on all his charm.

But even he was a bit surprised when the strictest Union agreed to his plans – reluctantly but without a fight. Kindly they agreed not to call a strike… just this once.

Then, when the biggest Concert Hall juggled its bookings to give him a space, the arrangements all fell into place.

Finally, after much careful plotting with his Publicity People, von Schnittlauch began rehearsals in secret.

The hunt for hidden talent was on.

STRICTLY NO ENTRY

REHEARSALS IN PROGRESS

Nobody had any idea what was happening but many people tried to guess. Soon amazing rumours spread throughout the musical world.

"It's a shocker," cried the newspapers. "Yobs play with Snobs."

All this drove the public wild. The tickets sold faster and faster.

Dr. Woodhead certainly didn't buy one but all the other important people who knew all about music just had to be there.

When the great day came, even the most critical critic arrived on time, smoking his biggest cigar.

Here indeed was a great authority on music. In his long career, there was nothing he hadn't seen and heard. There'd been people playing drain pipes, music for vacuum cleaners, string players in helicopters, even cellists with no clothes on. So, the prospect of a piece for cats and beginners did not turn a hair. But his critical pencil was as sharp as ever and he very much looked forward to writing a withering review.

"LADIES AND GENTLEMEN, PLEASE TAKE YOUR SEATS, THIS EVENING'S CONCERT IS ABOUT TO BEGIN…"

The work began with a gritty, infectious rhythm…the first of the special effects.

This was interrupted by a cascade of curious tones which grew more and more disturbing.

Then came the first notes from the specially trained choir. To recapture that splendid, subtle sound that had inspired Percy Nightingale so much…

…Bruno had trained all his brothers and sisters to sing in the dark.

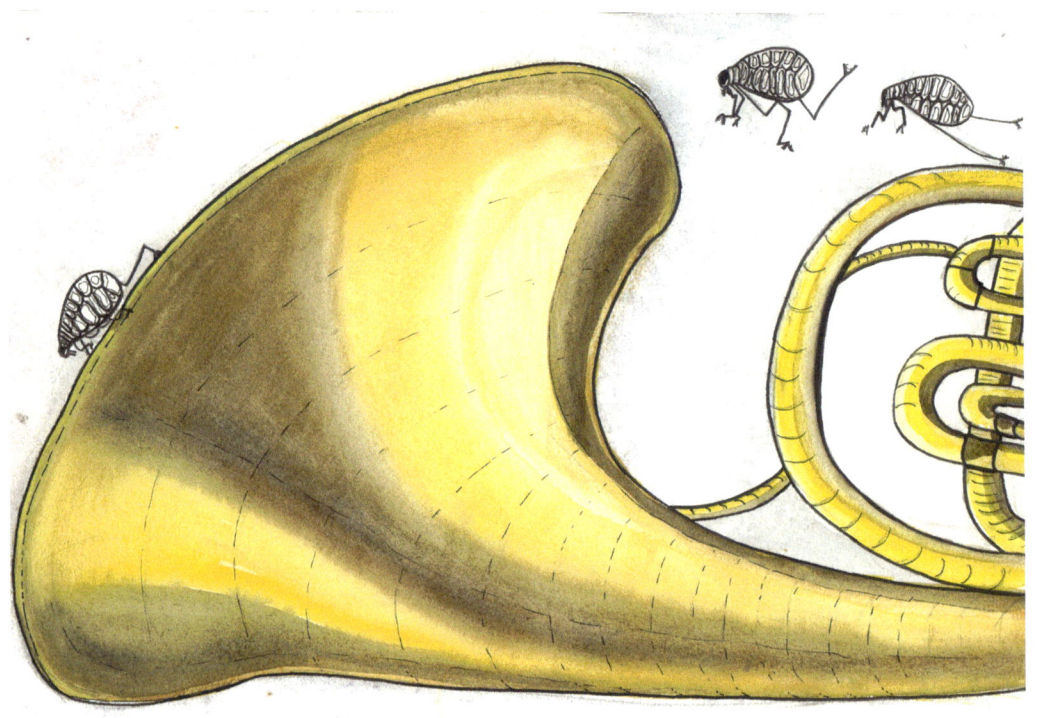

In came the horns with an acrobatic flourish. Their magnificent roar sent shivers through the hall. All the choir-fur stood on end so that even the laziest fleas began to stir. For some the enjoyment was purely musical…

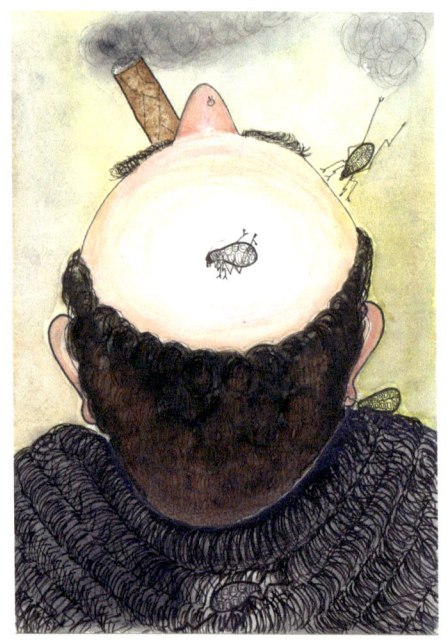

…others were more attracted by the refined flavours of such a well-dressed audience.

Poor Percy Nightingale was very nervous. He stood at the back of the hall clasping and unclasping his hands. He listened but he hardly dare look. All his life he'd waited for this moment...his whole reputation was at stake.

Everything depended on the orchestra, yet some of them had never appeared in a concert hall before. He remembered what von Schittlauch had told them in rehearsal. "Dear Colleagues, in this sublime new music, be brave. Every wrong note you play will be right...as long as you truly believe it!"

Percy shuddered. It was hair-raising. But he need not have worried. The old hands rose to the occasion, the actors mimed for their lives and, after so many weeks of training, even the complete beginners seemed transported. Their short sharp peculiar outbursts only made the fine playing of the true professionals sound even more magical.

The audience were open-mouthed, one moment shocked, then soothed, then deeply moved.

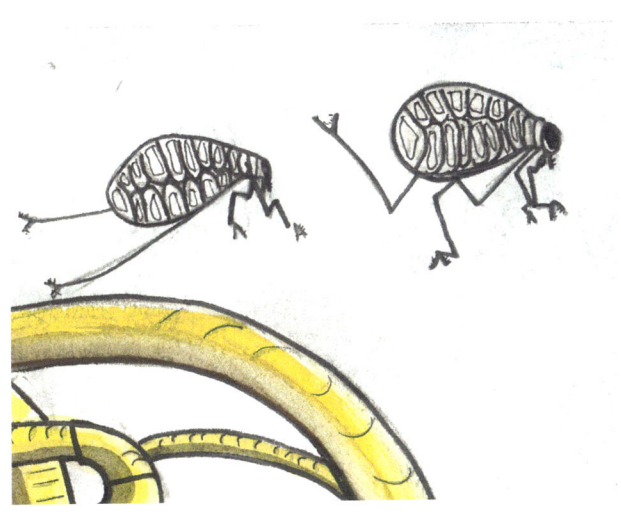

As for von Schnittlauch, he'd reached such a peak of fitness that his energy seemed to flood the hall.

Never had an orchestra seemed so inspired. Never had an orchestra faced such a challenge. Unable to sit still for a moment, they found that even when they weren't playing, they were spurred on by a strange itch.

Bravely they battled on as von Schnittlauch urged them into the finale. The music slowly built to a tremendous climax until at the very peak, when the tension was agonising, when orchestra and audience alike could bear it no longer, down came the dustbin lid again.

Then arose the pitiful, heartbreaking cries of the special choir. Bruno and friends began a gentle, poignant wailing that spread and wafted throughout the hall, bewitching every ear, before slowly fading away to a deathly, chilling silence.

The audience were overwhelmed. Many were moved to tears. Cheers and cries filled the hall. Excited fleas leapt higher and higher. Everyone was on their feet.

The power of great music had triumphed over adversity once again.

The cheering shocked and disturbed the critical critic almost as much as the music. This was not what he'd expected. The struggling crowds were so thick that he found it almost impossible to get out of the hall to the bar. He sweated, fumed and scratched. But seeing the twinkle in his girlfriend's eye, he did have to admit that **From Afar** might have a certain something after all.

"Air blowing from another planet?" teased his girlfriend with a knowing smile.

"Gattini animati? Novizi totali?"

"Hmm. Possibly, quite possibly," he sighed reluctantly under his breath.

"BRA–VO NIGHT–IN–GALE, BRA–VO NIGHT–IN–GALE!" shouted the audience, cheering and stamping their feet. The nervous Composer trembled to hear his name echoing through the hall for the first time in his life. He was longing to escape but von Schnittlauch knew better. He lingered in the spotlight just as long as he could. Such waves of applause were what he most adored. They kept him feeling young. Finally, back they went together to the dressing rooms. Percy could not thank his friend enough for such a magnificent performance. The great conductor was quite overcome.

Nevertheless, when he heard the pop of the champagne corks, he began to feel a little stronger. "…And how many ladies fainted?" he murmured.

Soon he was ready to join the celebrations and as a lover of good food, he was particularly struck by the special paté chosen for the occasion by his namesake.

"Quite unique!" he declared. "I've never tasted anything quite like it in my life."

    The excitement lasted all night. When Percy and Bruno finally arrived home it was already getting light and they could hardly recognise their own front door. Wearily, they pushed aside the piles of flowers and left the post unopened on the floor.

Percy Nightingale was just about to fall into bed when there was a knock on the door, then another. All the reporters were falling over each other to be the first to ask him what it felt like to be famous.

It felt terrible. The wine, the roses, the paté, the excitement, the crowds, not to mention the fear of failure…it had all been far too stressful after such a quiet and regular life.

Standing on the landing outside his flat, Percy was almost asleep on his feet – but then he got the most awful shock.

Amidst all the excitement, Bruno's gang had found their way back and could resist the Laundry Box no longer.

The cameras were rolling, the cats were fighting, the neighbour's sheets were in awful danger. Once again they would be ruined. Faced with such a crisis, Percy Nightingale sprang across the landing. Somehow he had to rescue the laundry. Nothing less than a masterly display of cat control would do.

The reporters were delighted. It gave them just the photos they needed to match their headlines.

"Catophonic Concert a sensation."

"What a purrformance."

"Purrfect Mewsick!"

"Cats score a hit!" the papers would cry.

But Percy was too tired to care. He closed the door and fell into bed. He slept…

…and slept…

… and slept.

Percy had never had such an exciting time in all his life and nor had Bruno.

No wonder they both needed such a long deep sleep to recover. But who can say what filled their dreams?

Was it the sound of an even grander piece of music… another extravaganza from afar? Or was it the scent of paté and roses, the flowers and the cheers? Or was it merely the clattering of cups and the smell of toasted teacakes, the rewards for a good day's work?

All we can say is that finally Percy Nightingale became a proper Composer at last. His dream came true, helped along by the two Brunos in his life. One was a conductor with flare, the other was his special assistant who put paws on scores with such care.

THE END